YOUR KNOWLEDGE HAS VALUE

- We will publish your bachelor's and
  master's thesis, essays and papers

- Your own eBook and book -
  sold worldwide in all relevant shops

- Earn money with each sale

Upload your text at www.GRIN.com
and publish for free

Aldridge Menzel

CPLM Blue Ocean Strategy

GRIN Verlag

Bibliografische Information der Deutschen Nationalbibliothek:

Die Deutsche Bibliothek verzeichnet diese Publikation in der Deutschen National-
bibliografie; detaillierte bibliografische Daten sind im Internet über http://dnb.d-
nb.de/ abrufbar.

Imprint:

Copyright © 2011 GRIN Verlag GmbH
Druck und Bindung: Books on Demand GmbH, Norderstedt Germany
ISBN: 978-3-656-62560-5

This book at GRIN:

http://www.grin.com/en/e-book/270839/cplm-blue-ocean-strategy

CPLM Blue Ocean Strategy

Table of Contents

Introduction

This paper is an attempt to explore the Blue Ocean Strategy which surfaced in the year 2004 and within a few months, it revolutionised thinking patterns and decision making processes of many firms around the world. The terms "red oceans" and "blue oceans" became the part of the business dictionary and many business related journals started using these terms.

It links to the themes of "critical response" and "critical thinking" because the very creation of Blue Ocean Strategy is a challenge or disapproval of the entire field of strategic management, the field of study which has been studied, explored and discussed by many well-known authors over the past five decades and even before that. Where strategic management has been constantly emphasising to outclass the competition, blue ocean strategy cites this approach as short minded and insufficient and instead, preaches the creation of blue oceans to make the competition irrelevant. The reasons why authors of this strategy came up with the blue ocean strategy was because the engaged in the process of critical thinking and critical response and gathered the courage to challenge the mainstream and widely held assumptions about competition. Despite the fact that concepts of innovation and creativity did exist before the advent of blue ocean strategy, Blue Ocean Strategy provided the business and an academic world with a new lens to look at innovation, creativity and value creation (Thompson & Strickland, pp. 314-316, 2003). When as of today, there are many scholars which disagree to the theory as cite it as irrelevant, inconsistent and not having enough theoretical and research grounding. On the other hand, there are scholars who are engaged in the process of defending the theory thus creating an ongoing process of dialogue, critical thinking and critical response. The paper also explores those criticisms and makes an attempt to provide the answers for them.

Discussion

Meaning of Blue and Red Oceans

Red and blue oceans represent the entire market universe. At any given point in time, the sum of markets would be equal to the sum of red and blue oceans. The names given to them are based on their certain characteristics which are discussed below.

Rather than remaining concerned with playing by the rules, firms in blue oceans create their own rules. In red oceans, the strategy created by firms flows from the industry structure. Interestingly, in blue oceans, the structure of the newly born industry is shaped by the strategy of the company (Thompson & Strickland, pp. 314-316, 2003). All concepts of competition, competitors, wars, rivalry and others become completely irrelevant. Within red oceans, when the firms have an option for either going for low cost "or" differentiation, in blue oceans, these firms can go for both low cost "and" differentiation strategies. In blue oceans, firms do not try to capture the demand but they create new demand for new products and services (Kim & Mauborgne, pp. 2-6, 2004).

Red Oceans

Red oceans or in other words, the known market place, refers to the market universe which is in existence today. The boundaries, limitations, rules and regulations within these red oceans are well defined and well known to the industry players. Here, the only way to expand the share of the market is to steal the market share of the other players thus inducing cut throat competition (Kim & Mauborgne, pp. 63-64, 2005). Firms which are present in red oceans are more likely to engage in price wars, aggressive marketing, heavy promotional campaigns and rivalry which have cost these firms trillions of dollars, all in the pursuit of beating one another but towards the end of the day, they are at the same level. Supply is most likely to exceed demand in these industries thus inducing firms to fight.

Blue Ocean Strategy

Blue ocean strategy argues that rather than wasting all your resources in fighting with the competition, one should engage in activities with which the competition could be made irrelevant. In fact, the authors even argue that the best method to beat competition is to stop trying to beat competition. As mentioned earlier that rather than playing by a predetermined set of rules, the blue ocean strategy argues that firms should redirect their limited resources in creating their own fields and own rules. Blue ocean strategy argues that "permanently great company" or "permanently great industry" is just a myth and it does not exist in reality. In the short term, companies and industries may benefit from booms, business cycles, environmental factors and other reasons but that does not last for long. However, what does exist is "permanently great strategic moves" (Kim & Mauborgne, p. 6, 2004).

In order to understand the importance of blue oceans, let us have a look at the changing industry structure or Porter Five Forces Model, in general, for most of the industries that are operating in the red oceans. Michael Porter, one of the most renowned thinkers and scholars of strategic management proposed his model would help in understanding that why some industries have above average profitability levels and others do not. Porter believed that it is due to the difference in industry structures which is made of five important competitive forces. These are threats of competitive rivalry, bargaining power of suppliers, bargaining power of customers, threat of substitute products and threat of new entrants. These competitive forces eat up the profitability of industries and when they are high, like in case of airline and book industry, profitability levels are low and when these forces are benign, like in case of the soft drink and pharmaceutical industry, the profitability levels are high (Kim & Mauborgne, pp. 2-6, 2004).

Threat of competitive rivalry refers to the degree to which companies face the threat of engaging in rivalries and wars. As mentioned earlier that when firms engage in rivalries, the industry always loses and the ultimate winner is mostly suppliers or the customers. Over the past few years, almost every other industry has seen a rise in the competitive rivalry due to the powerful force of globalisation and the advent of the internet. First, the number of rivals in every industry has increased thus leading to overcrowding. Gone are the days when companies had their own defined geographical regions where they would serve their customers. Today, with globalizing forces and internet, firms have expanded their geographical scope. In the 1960s and before, American automakers GM, Ford and Chrysler were fighting for three big companies in the automotive industry of the United States. However, today, these American automakers have to fight for market share with companies such as Toyota, Honda, Suzuki, BMW, Mercedes and others which are of Non-American origin (Gondek, pp. 85-89, 2011). The fact is that even a small company today can serve customers sitting thousands of miles away with the help of the internet. Therefore, every firm is now facing competition virtually from every other firm on the globe. Markets are open, trade barriers have been reduced thus overcrowding almost every industry. Second, industries in red oceans fail to enjoy any fast growth. Instead, they can be characterized by markets which are growing at a decreasing rate, declining or saturating. This is true because these organisations are not providing any radically new product or service but they are serving the same set of consumers with the same products and services, although, those products and services may be with little differences. Therefore, these industries where growth is slow or not happening, industry players are more likely to fight for their own share of pie. Depending on the degree to which any firm have aspirations of becoming the market leader, dependence on industry sales and fixed investments, the rivalry may even turn ugly, so much that the firms may even accept at operating their business at losses in order to force other firms out of the business (Kim & Mauborgne, pp. 2-6, 2004).

Bargaining Power of Customers in Red Oceans

Industries in which the bargaining power of customers is high, companies suffer greatly because buyers negotiate for prices, demand better services and quality, as much as possible, leaving the companies with smaller profit margins. Over the years, the bargaining power of buyers has increased greatly. First, as mentioned earlier that the scope of competition and industries is expanding, thus leaving customers with more choices and allowing them to dictate their terms. Second, many businesses are going online or having some sort of online presence, customers now have more information about prices, features and characteristics of the product thus allowing them to play each industry player against the other (Kim & Mauborgne, pp. 63-64, 2005). It is no longer simple to deceive customers expecting that they would not know about the offerings of other competitors. Third, buyer power would keep on increasing in the red oceans because of little differentiation between the products and services of different rivals. Although, companies may try their level best to come up with strong differences and value addition technique, being in the same red oceans mean that the competitors would quickly try to copy those changes and techniques and offer the same to customers. A few decades ago, intimidation took time as information transfer took time however, today, when information transfers in less than a second, transportation is quick and all the technology is available at the disposal, a rival may come up with the same product or service within a few hours (Hitt, et al., pp. 245-248, 2009).

Bargaining Power of Suppliers in Red Oceans

Bargaining power of suppliers, the flip side of bargaining power of customers can also be disastrous for any organisation. When suppliers become powerful, they demand higher prices, refuse to improve quality and cooperate completely and worse; they may even go for forward integration and end up becoming a competitor. Bargaining power of suppliers in red oceans is more likely to increase quickly because of the fact that for the creation of the same products and services, companies operating in the red oceans would have developed their dependence and partnerships with the suppliers thus increasing their switching costs. When suppliers are aware of the fact that the industry may face high switching costs in changing their services, they will feel more powerful. Furthermore, now with the help of the internet, suppliers have more access to the end consumers thus increasing the probability of forward integration from the side of suppliers (Kim & Mauborgne, pp. 2-6, 2004).

Industries which are profitable, relative to the other industries that are present in the red oceans, will attract new entrants. These new entrants will try to eat away the limited market share of the existing competitors. Furthermore, new entrants may raise the bar of quality and service in the industry thus increasing costs for everyone. Therefore, firms create barriers in order to keep away new entrants to enter in the industry. However, in the past few decades, the barriers of entry, in general, have decreased greatly (Hitt, et al., pp. 245-248, 2009). First, with the rise of online business, the level of fixed or initial investment to enter into any industry has decreased significantly. Most industries can have online businesses that can be set up with minimum investments. Second, many large companies would block the new entrants from entering with occupying the distribution, supplier and marketing channels. However, the internet has changed the rules of competition in many industries. Small businesses may make the internet as their marketing and distribution channel and firms may have nothing to do about the same (Kim & Mauborgne, pp. 2-6, 2004).

Threat of substitutes refers to the degree to which substitute and alternative products are attractive to the customers. Industries and companies operating in the red oceans are more likely to have substitutes because of their long presence and dominance which induces others to come up with different options. Historically, substitutes have existed for many products and services but customers have not known about most of them but in the digital age of today, much is known about these substitutes (Witcher & Chau, pp. 74-76, 2010).

Important here to note is that these are not the only challenges that are faced by the companies that operate in red oceans. The above mentioned paragraphs just give a glance at general challenges that arise from the choice of operating within red oceans. There could be a long list of industry specific competitive forces that various companies face. For example, the airline industry faces the challenge of high fixed investments which fuels the rivalry within industry. The industries that deal with food and grocery items are more likely to be selling products that are perishable thus forcing them to engage in price wars and promotional wars to sell their products quickly. In short, firms that are operating in red oceans are simultaneously facing many competitive forces eating away their profitability. The very survival of these firms is at stake. They have to settle for below average profits and never ending struggle for survival (Kim & Mauborgne, pp. 63-64, 2005).

In order to understand the basics of strategic management, consider the following story which is just the perfect manifestation of the grounding of this field of management. Once two company presidents, while considering a possible merger of the two companies, decided to go on a little picnic away from the city. As they discussed the matters of the merger while watching the beauty of the nature, they hiked deeper in the forest. They stopped suddenly and looked at each other. Both presidents knew that they have heard the grizzling of a bear. Before they could even react, they saw the bear appearing out of nowhere, standing in front of them on two feet as if he was challenging them. It all happened so quick that they mind could not process the possible reaction, however, one president realised that the other was opening his bag, took out his jogging shoes and changed his slippers quickly. The other president shouted that what are you doing? You cannot outrun a bear! The other president, all set to run in the other direction said "I know i can not outrun the bear. I just have to outrun you" (Henry, pp. 19-23, 2009)

Strategic management is all about beating, outclassing and doing better than the competition or competitors. Even when it tells you to come up strategy, vision, mission, goals and objectives; all of then must be directed at beating the competition. The authors of Blue Ocean Strategy believe that they very language of corporate strategy concepts represents military based thinking. For example, Chief Executive "officers" in "headquarters" and "troops" on the "front lines" (Hitt, et al., pp. 245-248, 2009). This explains why all strategies aim at "fighting" with rivals to such an extent that they could be driven out of the battlefield. These strategy follow a "do or die" thinking where you have to starve the opponent to death and there is no other choice. Every other theory, model or concept in strategic management urges or lays down a framework to engage in processes, activities, approaches and systems that are better than that of the competitors. They all urge to measure the performance of the company on a relative basis. If a company has grown by 25 percent within a certain period and the industry has grown by 35 percent during that period then the performance of the company will be cited as "unsatisfactory" because it was below average relative to the competition (Boyer & Verma, pp. 102-103, 2009). However, if during a certain period, a firm has recorded a negative growth of 10 percent and the entire industry at the same time has shrank by 20 percent then the firm would receive praise and appreciation for its performance. In addition, at the heart of strategic management lies the concept of competitive advantage. In simple terms, competitive advantage refers to something that a firm does better than the rival firms. Strategic management reinforces the concept of sustaining and maintaining competitive advantages so that customers could have a reason for selecting your firm over your competitors (Henry, pp. 19-23, 2009).

Criticisms and Misunderstandings about Blue Oceans

Most of the criticisms that blue ocean strategy receives is the result of many misunderstandings surrounding the strategy. This is the reason why the critics of blue ocean strategy cite it as "not working" or having a "weak grounding". First, critics of blue ocean strategy claim that many companies that have constantly launched new products, adopted new technologies and aimed for diversification of business have not been able to earn above average profits. In fact, many of these firms have failed miserably. The problem here is that they blue ocean is not about new products, new technologies and diversification of business (Witcher & Chau, pp. 74-76, 2010; Hitt, et al., pp. 245-248, 2009). A new product launch could simply be an extension of the previous product or a fine update of the product. A new technology could be a complete mismatch or misfit for the industry. Furthermore, diversification of any company could merely be an attempt to enter into a already existing red ocean. Blue Ocean and red ocean do not have the relationship of "new and old" but the difference between is of strategic movies. Blue oceans are not merely based on "innovation" but on "value innovation", something that could demand from the side of the buyers. New technology is not necessary for blue oceans (Boyer & Verma, pp. 102-103, 2009). Consider the example of mutual funds industry which did not require any technology. Furthermore, great companies like Starbucks and Cirque du Soleil also did not need any new technological breakthrough to become what they are in their respective markets. Blue oceans are about reconstructing the existing boundaries to create new buyer demand by providing them with value never provided to them before (Kim & Mauborgne, pp. 8, 2004).

Second, there are critics who label blue ocean strategy as an extremely defensive and cowardly as it preaches to evade competitions by changing businesses whenever the competition appears to be intensifying. They tell firms that blue ocean strategy is a shortcut to save themselves from the threat of competition, whereas, the right way to go about is to face the competition. Once again, they make a serious mistake in understanding blue ocean strategy. It is not necessarily about coming out of a particular industry but it is about reconstructing the boundaries to provide value innovation, as mentioned earlier (Kim & Mauborgne, pp. 19, 2005). Blue ocean strategy does not dictate firms to leave the red oceans. Surviving in red oceans is a part of the business as well but in order to find above average profitability, firms will have to find uncontested market places. Cirque du Soleil, when faced with a tough time, did not leave the circus industry, in fact, it went on to redefine the industry and reconstruct the boundaries. With its gadgets and computers, Apple has creating blue oceans but it did not have to leave the business for the same. When, in the 1970s, IBM came up with Personal Computers, it was not a shift in terms of industry but it was an approach for value creation and innovation (Dubrin, pp. 412-413, 2011).

Third, some critics of Blue Ocean believe that while blue ocean strategy appears to be promising, it is sustainable as any blue ocean would quickly turn into a red ocean due to the entry of many rivals who would see a new promising prospect. However, blue oceans may turn red over the period of time but the same is not possible in the short term. This is true because blue oceans are a result of a process and they are not merely market outcomes. Companies that truly follow the strategy will not only provide excellent services to the buyers but it also decrease the cost and price with the passage of time to create barriers and appeal to the masses (Hill & Jones, pp. 185-186, 2009; Boyer & Verma, pp. 102-103, 2009).

Examples of Blue Ocean Strategy

The corporate world is full of examples of blue ocean strategy. There are many firms that have, time and time again, reaped the advantages of going to uncontested market spaces and untapped customers groups.

Consider the example of Southwest Airlines, which has remained one of the most successful airlines in the US industry for the past decade or so. When in early 1970s, its founders, Rollin King and Herb Kelleher started the airline service, rather than benchmarking the competition and beating them, they came up with their own idea. They believed that if you take people from with one destination to the other with the minimum possible fares, they will fly your airline (Hill & Jones, pp. 185-186, 2009). Unlike other competitors, Southwest took out all the lavish and unnecessary expenditures by other airline and focused on the technical requirements. It minimised the facilities only to the ones that could be provided with minimum costs and paid attention on training the employees in such a way that it could help in implementing the low cost strategy. Not only people fly with Southwest airlines but they also enjoy it as it ranks highest in terms of customer satisfaction (Kim & Mauborgne, pp. 63-64, 2005; Dubrin, pp. 412-413, 2011).

Cirque Du Soliel is one of the most frequently cited examples in this regard which implemented the blue ocean strategy in the declining circus industry. It was the time when people were looking for alternative forms of entertainment within their homes and children were more interested in play stations, PCs and other gadgets rather than looking at clowns and animals in the circus. The supplier power of the animal owners and the performers was huge and so was the bargaining power (Kim & Mauborgne, pp. 12, 2005). Furthermore, the animal rights groups were seriously hurting the business with their campaigns. The already present players in the industry were fighting for the declining market share with their own scaled down versions. However, Cirque Du Solleil did not make an attempt to win back the customers from other competitors; instead it attracted a whole new group of customers, corporate clients and adults to circus with redefining the definition of entertainment. These customers were ready to pay a premium price for the services. The company expanded quickly and did the same in a decade what took the industry leaders to do in over a century (Kim & Mauborgne, pp. 63-64, 2005).

Conclusion

Blue ocean strategy does not dictate that firms should altogether quit their presence in red oceans. Being in red oceans and competing within is a part of the business world and every just have to accept it. However, if any firm wants to grow quickly, earn more profits and get rid of the competition for a long time then those firms should try to explore for blue oceans at the same time. Blue ocean strategy does not only have a qualitative grounding but it also based on quantitative facts. In fact, the study based on a decade long research of 108 companies that have lived during the past century from 30 different industries and comprising of 150 different moves. The study found out that over 86% of the new product launches were line extensions, which indicates increase in the size of red oceans. However, they only represented for over 62% of the total revenues earned by the firms during this firm and even less, a mere 39% of the profits. On the other hand, the rest of the 14% were product launches that allowed those firms to get out of the red oceans and reach the blue oceans. These generated almost 38% of the total income and 61% of the total profits (Gondek, pp. 85-89, 2011). These facts and figures, reinforce the points made in the paper that while firms may able to survive in red oceans with average or below average profits, in order to earn above average profits, firms will have to look for new, uncontested, unexplored and untapped blue oceans. They not only provide new lives to companies but they also play an important in creating an innovative and creative society with progressive attitudes and increasing standard of living for everyone (Hill & Jones, pp. 185-186, 2009).

References

Boyer, Kenneth Karel., & Verma, Rohit. 2009. *Operations and supply chain management for the 21st century*. Cengage Learning.

Dubrin, Andrew J. 2011. *Essentials of Management*. Cengage Learning.

Gondek, Christian. 2011. *Blue Ocean Strategy - An Insight Into the Future of Customer Relationship Management*. GRIN Verlag.

Henry, Anthony. 2008. *Understanding Strategic Management*. New York: Oxford University Press.

Hill, Charles., & Jones, Gareth. 2009. *Strategic Management Theory: An Integrated Approach*. Connecticut: Cengage Learning.

Hitt, Michael A., et.al. 2009. *Strategic management: competitiveness and globalization : concepts & cases*. Connecticut: Cengage Learning.

Kim, W. Chan., & Mauborgne, Renée. 2004. Rollin King and Herb Kelleher. *Harvard Business Review,* October 2004, pp. 1-9

Kim, W. Chan., & Mauborgne, Renée. 2005. *Blue Ocean Strategy: How to Create Uncontested Market Space and Make Competition Irrelevant*. Harvard Business Press.

Thompson, Arthur A., & Strickland, Alonzo J. 2003. *Strategic management: concepts and cases*. New York: McGraw-Hill/Irwin.

Wit, Bob De., & Meyer, Ron. 2010. *Strategy: Process, Content, Context, An International Perspective*. Connectcuit: Cengage Learning EMEA (Wit & Meyer, pp. 76-78

Witcher, Barry J., & Chau, Vinh Sum. 2010. *Strategic Management: Principles and Practice*. Cengage Learning EMEA.